Finish It

with ALEX ANDERSON

- 6 Quilt Projects
- Choose the Perfect Border
- Options for Edges

C&T PUBLISHING

Text and Artwork © 2004 Alex Anderson
Artwork © 2004 C&T Publishing

EDITORS: Liz Aneloski
TECHNICAL EDITORS: Joyce Engels Lytle and Pat Wilens
COPYEDITOR/PROOFREADER: Darra Williamson/Stacy Chamness
COVER DESIGNER: Kristen Yenche
BOOK DESIGN/PAGE LAYOUT: Maureen Forys, Happenstance Type-O-Rama
DESIGN DIRECTOR: Dave Nash
ILLUSTRATOR: Richard Sheppard
QUILT PHOTOGRAPHY: Sharon Risedorph
HOW-TO PHOTOGRAPHY: Diane Pedersen
COVER PHOTO STYLING: Diane Pederson and Garry Gay
COVER PHOTOGRAPHY: Garry Gay

Published by C&T Publishing, Inc., P.O. Box 1456, Lafayette, California, 94549

Library of Congress Cataloging-in-Publication Data
Anderson, Alex.
Finish it with Alex Anderson : 6 quilt projects, choose the perfect border,
options for edges.
    p. cm.
Includes an index.
ISBN 1-57120-256-0 (paper trade)
1. Quilting—Patterns. 2. Patchwork—Patterns. I. Title.

TT835.A51697 2004
746.46—dc22

2004001089

Printed in China

10 9 8 7 6 5 4 3 2 1

■ Table of Contents

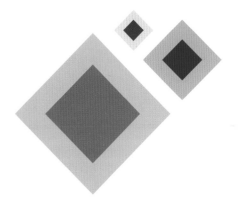

■ Acknowledgments

Thank you to:

Paula Reid and *Elizabeth Scott*, who worked creatively side by side with me throughout the creation of this book. It was a pleasure combining creative talents and technical skills with you.

Darra Williamson, who kept this book on track through my summer of kitchen/home renovation.

Moda, *Free Spirit Fabrics*, *P&B Textiles*, and *Robert Kaufman Fabrics*, who so graciously provided such wonderful fabric to work with—and then some!

Bernina, for letting me create and play on their terrific sewing machines.

Olfa Products, for great tools to create with.

My creative team at C&T, who always promise excellence in the final results…

…and *YOU*, the reader, who continues to inspire and motivate me.

■ Dedication

Darra, I thank you from the bottom of my heart. This book would not have been possible without your friendship and guidance.

Introduction

I love making quilts, all the way from the first spark of an idea to placing my signature on the back.

Designing and creating a quilt is a fascinating process that keeps us quiltmakers on our toes. From fabric to finishing, there are so many decisions to make! In some ways, making a quilt is like parenting a child: your best intentions for them may not be the road *they* choose. This doesn't necessarily mean things go down the wrong path, just a different one than you expected. You might think your quilt is going to finish a certain way, but when it's time for the border and binding, the quilt says, "No, let's go another direction."

Irish Nine-Patch (page 36) is a perfect example, Both Elizabeth (who pieced it) and I were convinced that an appliquéd swag border was the answer for this quilt. In fact, the quilt was designed and pieced for this. Surprise! The quilt took on a life of its own. Paula's beautiful, subtle quilting in variegated rayon thread became the only and obvious choice. The results were both surprising and stunning.

In short, we just need to consider our quilts as teammates, and let the quilts take the lead. Yes, it's true: quilts do have minds of their own!

This book was written to give you ideas and options for finishing up your quilts. Borders, bindings, and other edgings have their own set of design considerations and style of application. My wish is that you'll use this book as inspiration and instruction when considering your borders and finishes. There are many options available to us as quiltmakers. It is simply a matter of considering ideas and having the instruction to implement your plan.

Producing the quilts for this book was a cooperative effort. In need of assistance (due to time restrictions), I called upon two very talented ladies, who also happen to be my friends. Elizabeth Scott helped with the creation of several of the quilt tops and Paula Reid creatively quilted life into most of the pieces (I had the delicious joy of hand quilting *Scrappy Triangles*, page 44.) We worked together and designed as a team under my direction. Never having worked this way before I was delightfully surprised how exciting the process was. The intention of this book was of course to highlight the use of great borders and bindings. Not surprisingly, each quilt took on it's own personality. When one person became frustrated or stumped, another would step in to save the day. The creation of this book was an incredibly fun experience for all of us. We all have special gifts and talents to share. Our craft has been handed so graciously from one person to another throughout history and this was a positive example of this. I am grateful for this experience with Elizabeth and Paula. I look forward to working this way again.

Tools and Supplies

Most of the tools and supplies you'll need for stitching borders and achieving "fine finishes" are probably already in your sewing room. Here are some of my thoughts about the basics.

Fabric: 100% cotton is the fabric of choice for most quilters—including me!—and I recommend you use the very best quality you can find. Believe me, you'll be pleased with the results: good quality cotton handles well for accurate cutting and piecing, turns under nicely for appliqué, and stands up well to laundering and use.

Opinions differ as to whether or not you should prewash your fabric. My vote is a resounding "yes," and here's why. Cotton can shrink when washed for the first time, so prewashing eliminates the potential for puckers and distortion in your finished quilt. It can also remove excess dye, or alert you to unstable color that can "bleed" or "run" when your quilt is washed later. Finally, prewashing removes any chemical residue introduced in the manufacturing process.

Thread: Use a quality cotton thread. Neutral gray or tan works great for piecing. For invisible hand appliqué, choose a color to match the appliqué piece, and for buttonhole appliqué, try embroidery floss (I like to use two-ply) or perle cotton thread in a contrasting color.

Pins: You'll be sewing lots of long seams as you add borders, bindings, and other finishing treatments, so don't be tempted to skimp here! Invest in extra-fine (1⅜″/0.50mm) glass-head pins. I love them both for machine piecing and for appliqué. They may cost a bit more at the outset, but they are worth it in successful results. Trust me on this: using inferior-quality, bargain brand pins will only cause you headaches!

Tape Measure: Keep one handy to measure your quilt top for borders. A metal one works best, since fabric tapes can stretch and become inaccurate over time.

Rotary Cutter: I can't imagine cutting borders or bindings without my trusty rotary cutter! The medium-size cutter can cut up to four layers of 100% cotton at once, while the larger cutter cuts through six layers easily and quickly. If you're purchasing a rotary cutter for the first time, and your budget allows, treat yourself to the larger size. Otherwise, the medium size will do fine.

Rotary Ruler: Choose a ruler that is up to the task of cutting large pieces and long strips. The 6″ × 24″ size Omnigrid or Olfa are excellent choices, particularly for borders. They are ideally sized, marked both horizontally and vertically in ⅛″ increments, and identify the 45° angle you'll need for perfect mitered corners.

Rotary Mat: These self-healing wonders are designed specifically for use with rotary cutters. Although you can make do with a smaller size, the larger varieties (*e.g.*, 24″ × 36″) are great for cutting large border strips.

Iron: You probably already own an iron suitable for quiltmaking, but eventually you'll want to invest in a super-hot steam iron. Successful pressing is an important step in creating a well-crafted quilt!

Sewing Machine: You'll want those nice, long seams to go—well!—seamlessly. Be sure your machine is in good working condition, with proper tension, an even stitch, and a sharp size 80 needle.

Border Basics

Think of your quilt's border as a frame, setting off your quilt to its best advantage. Take time to decide how many and what kind of borders to use, and what fabrics to make them with. These decisions are important to the success of your quilt: the beauty of even the most wonderful painting can be diminished by a poor choice of frame.

To be successful, the border needs to relate or add something to the quilt's overall design. In short, it needs to make sense visually. Use it to repeat or emphasize a key color, fabric, shape, block, or other element in the body (center) of the quilt.

A design wall is invaluable in deciding how to border quilts. Use it to audition border ideas, including how wide to make the borders, and to choose which fabrics to use.

> My design wall consists of large sheets of Celotex (typically available at home supply stores and lumber yards) mounted to the wall and covered with white flannel, but something as simple as a length of white cotton batting, felt, or flannel taped or tacked to the wall works just fine.

Quilts sometimes have borders on just two or three sides, or the borders are all cut from different fabrics, or the top and bottom borders are wider (or narrower) than the side borders. There is no "rule" that says a quilt must have four identical borders, so don't be afraid to experiment.

Sometimes you'll discover your quilt doesn't need any border at all. That's what happened with *Butterfly* (page 40). Once the pieced side triangles were in place, the design seemed complete, so the quilt was finished with prairie points, and that was that!

▦ Border Proportions

Design Considerations

While there is no set "rule" for sizing borders, consider the size of the blocks, as well as the overall body of the quilt, and keep the borders in reasonable proportion. *Never use a border just to enlarge your quilt.* It may seem like an easy way to stretch a minimum number of blocks, but you will likely regret it afterwards. The borders will overpower the quilt, and—trust me!—your strategy will be obvious. Instead, make those few extra blocks, or try an alternative setting to maximize the blocks at hand. Your quilt is worth the extra effort!

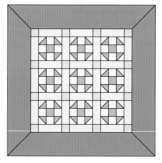 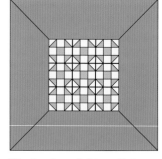

This quilt has pleasing proportions.

The border of this quilt is too large for the size and number of blocks used.

Many quilts, including most of mine, have more than one border. The inner border is usually small in relation to the outer border(s), much like an inner mat on a picture frame. It can give the eye a great resting place in a quilt's design, and—on occasion—come in handy for making minor "math adjustments" between the body of the quilt and its outer borders. In addition, a pieced inner border can add visual interest to a "quiet" quilt.

If you decide to use multiple borders, vary their widths. Go from narrow, to wider, to wider still, or from narrow, to wider, to narrow again. Your quilt will feel less "rigid"—and be more appealing. Once again, proportion is the key.

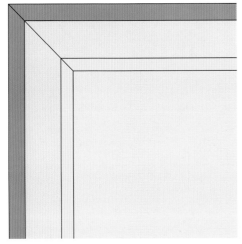

Vary border widths.

Intended Use

My quilts are often made for the wall, so adapting borders to accommodate a bed usually isn't a factor. However, when making a quilt for a bed, it's common to design the body of the quilt to cover the mattress top, and the border(s) to form the overhang (drop).

The typical drop for a bed-sized quilt is 10″ on three sides: left, right, and bottom. (If you have an extra-deep mattress, measure to make sure 10″ will cover it.) Some quilters also add 10″ to account for

the pillow, either by extending the design of the body of the quilt, by adding an extra wide sashing for a pillow tuck, or by adding a border to the top edge of the quilt as well.

■ Squaring Up the Quilt

If the corners of your quilt are less than perfectly "square," fix that *before* adding any borders. Use a large ruler to make sure the sides of your quilt top are straight, and each corner forms a perfect 90° angle. Use your rotary cutter to make any adjustments. Be careful not to trim off any important design elements (such as points) in the process!

Square up the quilt.

■ Measuring for Borders

It's not unusual for the edges of your quilt top to stretch a bit during the construction process. If you cut borders to match these slightly skewed outer-edge measurements, you'll end up with a bad case of "wavy borders."

To avoid this problem, measure your quilt *through its center*, both horizontally and vertically, rather than along its outside edges. Use these "true" measurements to cut the borders.

Cutting and Grainline

It's a good idea to cut border strips before cutting any of the other pieces for your quilt. That way, you're sure to have enough fabric, and won't need to piece odd leftovers to make the borders—or worse yet, discover there aren't enough leftovers to piece!

I allow a little extra length when pre-cutting border strips for my quilts. Then I can measure the completed quilt top and trim the strips to size when I'm ready to stitch them. The cutting instructions for each project in this book allow for additional length in the border strips.

You can cut border strips from either the lengthwise (parallel to the selvage) or crosswise (selvage to selvage) grain of the fabric.

To cut borders from the crosswise grain, you generally have to purchase less yardage. The slight give in the grain makes these borders easier to ease or gently stretch to fit than lengthwise-cut borders.

You may need to piece strips to get the necessary length. Nondescript, subtle, tone-on-tone, or random prints work best for seamed borders. If your border fabric has a very distinctive print that will make seams obvious, or if you just prefer borders without seams, purchase extra fabric and cut the borders from the lengthwise grain.

Certain fabrics are so obviously directional (e.g., some pictorial prints) you may wish to cut two borders on the crosswise grain, and two on the lengthwise grain so everything points "right side up." This may take additional yardage, which you'll want to know in advance…another good reason to audition fabrics on your design wall!

Whenever possible, I piece border strips with a diagonal seam. This distributes the visual "weight" of the seam, so it tends to be less obvious. I make an exception for borders cut from striped fabrics, where a straight seam is usually less noticeable.

To piece a diagonal seam:

1. Place two border strips right sides together, overlapping the ends at a 90° angle and allowing a ¼" overhang at the end of each strip.

2. Use a ruler to mark the 45° angle on the top strip.

3. Sew on the marked line to join the border strips.

4. Trim the excess fabric to a ¼" seam allowance, and press the seam open. If you are preparing bias strips, be careful not to stretch the strip.

5. Trim the "bunny ears" even with strip edge.

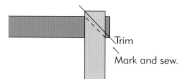

Piece the border strips.

Trim the "bunny ears."

Each border treatment has its own requirements for figuring border lengths. You'll find this information in the section describing each specific technique.

Stitching Borders

1. Find and mark the midpoint on each side edge of the quilt top and the midpoint of each border strip by folding in half and creasing lightly. For large quilts, mark additional points between the midpoints.

   For some border options—such as mitered borders (pages 9–11)—you'll also need to identify and mark the place where the border must match with the corner of the quilt top. This is noted in the section describing that option.

2. Place the border and the quilt top right sides together. Match and pin the midpoints, corners, and any key points you've marked. Fill in the "gaps" with *as many pins as you need* to distribute the fabric evenly, easing the quilt top to fit the border.

3. Stitch the border to the quilt top with a ¼″ seam. Check periodically to be sure you aren't stitching pleats into either the quilt top or the border.

> I sew with the layer (quilt top or border) that needs to be eased on the bottom, so the feed dogs gently assist the easing process. I remember it this way: larger side on the bottom...just like me!

4. Press the border seam. These seams are usually pressed away from the center of the quilt. Sometimes, however, they just want to go the other way, and I normally let the quilt take the lead.

> If your border requires a fair amount of easing, machine baste it to the quilt top first. Once you're sure you haven't stitched in any tucks, re-sew the border with a normal stitch and remove the basting. This also works great for adding pieced borders with lots of seams to match.

◾ Border Options

The design will dictate which of the following techniques to use.

Butted Borders

Borders with butted corners are the easiest borders to stitch. All the joining seams are straight—no angles—with the border seams forming a T at the corners where they meet.

I typically add the side borders first, then the top and bottom borders. I find this often saves fabric. It's not written in stone, however, so feel free to swap the sewing order if you wish. If you are following project

instructions, be sure to adjust the lengths of the borders accordingly.

1. Measure your quilt from top to bottom as described on page 7. Cut two border strips this length.

2. Fold the quilt top in half, top to bottom, to find and mark the midpoint along one side; repeat for a border strip. Place the quilt top and border strip right sides together, matching the midpoints, and pin.

3. Pin the ends of the border strip to the corners of the quilt top, and every 2″, easing or stretching slightly to fit. Sew with a ¼″ seam and press following the arrows. Repeat for the other side border.

4. Measure your quilt from side to side, including the borders you just added. Cut two borders to this length. Pin and sew to the top and bottom of the quilt the same way you did for the side borders; press following the arrows.

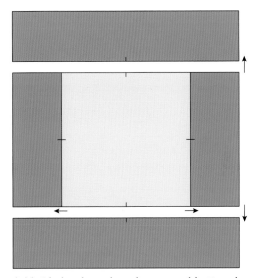

Add side borders, then the top and bottom borders.

Mitered Borders

Mitered borders have corner seams angled at 45° so the border corner truly resembles a picture frame. These borders are a little trickier, but the results are well worth the effort.

1. Measure your quilt top from top to bottom as described on page 7. Add two times the finished width of the border, plus an extra 2″–3″ for seam allowance and "insurance." Cut the side borders to this length.

2. Measure your quilt from side to side as described on page 7. Add two times the finished width of the border, plus an extra 2″–3″ for seam allowance and "insurance." Cut the top and bottom borders to this length.

3. Find and mark the midpoint on each side of the quilt top and the midpoint of each border strip as described in Stitching Borders (pages 8–9). From the marked midpoint, measure in both directions and mark half the *length* of the quilt top on each side border. Repeat, using the *width* of the quilt top to measure and mark the top and bottom borders.

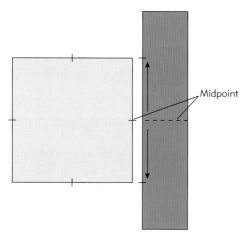

Midpoint

Measure and mark.

4. Place a side border and the quilt top right sides together. Match and pin the midpoints, and then the corners of the quilt top with the marked ends of the border strip. The border will extend beyond the edges of the quilt top. Use additional pins as needed.

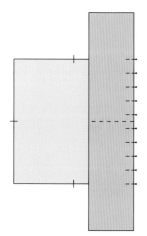

Match points and pin.

5. Stitch the border to the quilt top. Start and end the seam with a backstitch, ¼″ in from the corners of the quilt top. Press. Repeat for the other side, and the top and bottom borders.

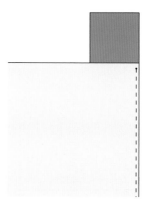

Stitch to within ¼″ of the corners.

6. Lay a corner of the quilt top right side up on your ironing board. Place one border strip on top of the neighboring border.

7. Fold the top border strip under, so it forms a 45° angle, and press lightly. Use a ruler with a 45° marking to check that the angle is accurate, and that the corner of the quilt is flat and square. Make any necessary adjustments. When you're sure everything is in place, firmly press the fold.

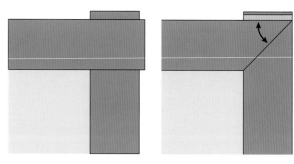

Place one border strip on top of the other.   **Fold the border strip at a 45° angle.**

8. From the corner, fold the quilt top on the diagonal, right sides together, aligning the long raw edges of the neighboring border strips. The fold you've made in the border should form a perfect extension of the diagonal fold in the quilt top. Mark the fold line with a pencil, and pin.

9. To sew the miter, backstitch at the inside corner, at the point where the border seams meet, then stitch along the marked fold toward the outside corner of the border. You'll be stitching on the bias, so be careful not to stretch the corner as you sew. Backstitch to finish.

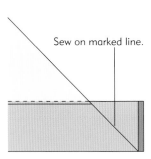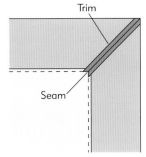

Fold the quilt top to align the fold lines. Sew.

Trim.

10. Trim the excess border fabric to a ¼" seam allowance, and press the seam open.

11. Repeat Steps 6–10 to miter the remaining corners.

> When adding multiple mitered borders, cut all borders to the length of the outside border. Sew the borders together, and stitch them to the quilt as a single unit. You'll only need to miter each corner once!

Partial-Seam Borders

This technique is sometimes used to construct blocks such as Around the Twist. The first border is partially stitched to the quilt, and finished after the last border is attached. The result is a quirky design twist that I particularly like for striped inner borders.

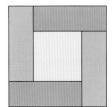

Around the Twist block

1. Measure your quilt from top to bottom as described on page 7. Add the finished width of the border, plus an extra ½" for seam allowances. Cut the side borders to this length.

2. Measure your quilt from side to side as described on page 7. Add the finished width of the border, plus an extra ½" for seam allowances. Cut the top and bottom borders to this length.

3. Find and mark the midpoint on each side of the quilt top as described in Stitching Borders (pages 8–9).

4. From one end of each side border, measure and mark the *length* of the quilt top. Find and crease the midpoint between the end of the strip and the point you've just marked. Repeat for the top and bottom borders, measuring and marking the *width* of the quilt top, and creasing to find the midpoint.

5. Place a side border and the right edge of the quilt top right sides together. Match the midpoints, and the bottom right corner of the quilt top with the marked endpoint on the border, and pin. (The border will extend beyond the bottom edge of the quilt.) Align the opposite end of the border strip with the top right corner of the quilt, and pin as needed.

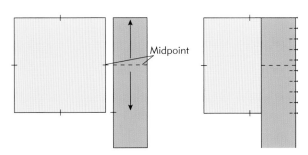

Measure and mark the length of the quilt top and midpoint.

Match the corners and marked points and pin.

6. Stitch the border strip to the quilt top, stopping approximately 3" from the corner of the quilt top. (See illustration on page 12.) Press.

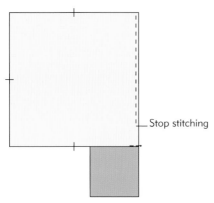

Stop stitching

Stitch, stopping approximately 3" from the corner.

7. Place the top border and the top edge of the quilt top right sides together. Match the midpoints, and the ends of the border with the corners of the quilt. Pin as needed.

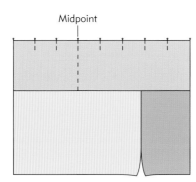

Midpoint

Match marked points and corners and pin top border.

8. Stitch the border to the quilt; press.

9. Repeat to add the left side and the bottom borders.

10. Complete the first border seam; press. If necessary, trim and square the corners of the quilt as described on page 7.

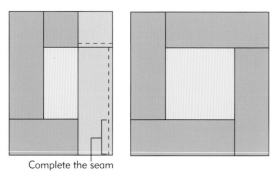

Complete the seam

Complete seam of first border.

Borders with Corner Squares

Borders with corner squares give a quilt a wonderful, traditional flavor. They are easy to sew, and—here's a little secret!—can come to your rescue if you run just a bit short of border fabric.

Cut them from a single fabric or from a variety of fabrics for a scrappy look. If you like, you can piece them as in *Amish Baskets* (page 29). Just be sure they relate to the rest of the quilt in color or design.

1. Measure your quilt top through the center from top to bottom as described on page 7. Cut two border strips this measurement for the side borders.

2. Repeat Step 1, this time measuring your quilt top from side to side for the top and bottom borders.

3. Stitch the side borders to the quilt top as described in Butted Borders on page 9.

4. Stitch corner squares onto both ends of the top and bottom borders; press.

5. Stitch to the top and bottom of the quilt, carefully matching the corner seams; press.

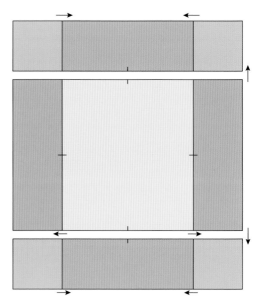

Stitch as shown and press following arrows.

Pieced Borders

You can make the simplest pieced borders by stitching scrappy strips of random length, as I did for the outer border of *Scrappy Triangles* (page 44). The mix of light print fabrics adds visual interest, and enhances the overall richness of the quilt's design.

A pieced border is a fabulous way to repeat or emphasize a key shape (or shapes) in the body of the quilt. For example, the pieced Sawtooth border of *Unknown Star* (page 33) echoes the many triangles in the large Star blocks, unifying the overall design.

Whenever possible, plan the finished size of your pieced border unit or block so it divides evenly into the finished measurements of your quilt top. If it doesn't, there *are* ways to cope!

One simple solution is to add (or adjust) an inner border to make up the difference. Another is to insert an appropriately sized "spacer" to make the necessary adjustment in the pieced border. This spacer can be a simple strip, or a specially designed unit or block relating to the quilt and border design. Center the spacer in the border, or place it randomly. If you wish, use it to change direction of the border units or blocks.

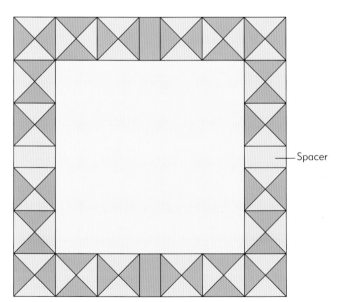

Add spacers to make border fit.

Turn corners by repeating the border unit or block, substituting (or designing) a special corner unit, or using simple corner squares like the ones in *Unknown Star* (page 33).

Self-Bordering Quilts

Rail Fence (page 26) creates its own border just by changing the value range of the blocks ringing the center of the quilt. The blocks in the center are lighter, and are made from fabrics in the light to medium range. Blocks made from medium-dark and dark fabrics surround the lighter blocks with just enough contrast to give the illusion of a border. Since the blocks are set on point, dark setting triangles complete the illusion.

This option works well with other straight-set quilts too. Experiment with changes in value, or color for all sorts of simple, but interesting, effects.

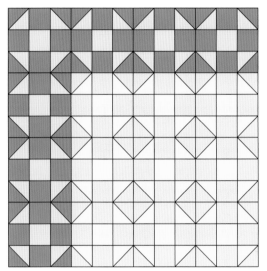

Change value to create border.

Scalloped Borders

Scalloped edges give a quilt an elegant, feminine finish. The scallops are marked after you've sewn the borders to the quilt, but before basting and quilting.

Marking Method One

Sometimes it will be left to you to determine the size of the scallop. In this case, you'll want to size the scallop so it divides evenly into the sides and the top and bottom edges of the quilt.

1. Divide one side of the quilt top into equal segments, and mark the divisions. Fold the opposite edge up to the marked side and repeat the markings. Do the same for the other sides.

2. Decide how *deep* you want the scallops to be and make registration marks. Trace a plate or something similar to mark the scallops.

3. Baste and quilt as usual, keeping any appliqué or quilting motifs within the marked scallops.

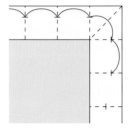

Marking Method Two

At other times, the size of the scallop will be determined by an appliqué or quilting design, as in *Irish Nine-Patch* on page 36.

1. Option 1: Mark the quilt top following the curve of the appliquéd scallops; then baste and quilt as usual.

2. Option 2: Baste and quilt a scalloped design. Mark the scalloped edge following the curve of the quilting design.

Appliqué and Quilted Borders

An appliqué border lends a pleasing touch of contrast to the geometry of a pieced quilt. As always, carry some element from the body of the quilt—color, shape, proportion—into the border so the overall design is visually connected. *Scrappy Triangles* (page 44) is a good example. The gentle curves of the appliqué border soften the sharp corners of the quilt's many triangles. Yet the design "holds together," since the piecework and appliqué shapes are similar in size and share many of the same fabrics. The appliqué vine "breaks the boundary" and crosses into the body of the quilt, making the connection even stronger.

Cut and fold lengths of freezer paper to match the border measurements and experiment with full-size appliqué designs. Or simply cut lengths of bias vine, flowers, leaves, and other pleasing shapes, and place the appliqués by eye for a whimsical, freeform look.

> The border is easier to appliqué before it is attached to the quilt top. Appliqué three-quarters of each border, leaving the corners to be finished once the borders are stitched to the quilt top.

If you wish, substitute quilting for appliqué in the borders of your quilt. Beautifully quilted cables, feathers, fans, and other curvy designs provide a nice contrast to the straight lines of patchwork. Keep the look subtle by matching thread color to the border fabric, or call attention to the quilting with fabulous colored threads. *Irish Nine-Patch* (page 37) features a quilted border that really shines: its graceful swag perfectly echoes the quilt's scalloped edge.

Edge-Finishing Basics

The purpose of any edge-finishing treatment is to enclose and protect the raw edges of a quilt's three layers. Depending upon how you plan to use your finished quilt, the edges can receive lots of wear and tear. This is one reason I do not recommend turning the backing to the front to create a self-binding.

In addition to being functional, finishing is a design decision as well. The treatment you select for your quilt is your final chance to make a statement, so make your choice carefully.

◼ Binding

The most common method of finishing a quilt is with an applied binding, which goes on *after the quilt is quilted*. Making your own binding gives you unlimited choices in color and fabric, and guarantees that the quality of the binding fabric matches the rest of the quilt.

There are several ways to make and apply binding. The best choice will depend upon your quilt's size, function, and design.

As with borders, I frequently rely on my design wall to audition bindings. I can experiment with various fabrics, and also get a sense for how wide I want the finished binding to be.

Straight-Grain vs. Bias Binding

Binding cut on the straight grain—preferably crosswise—is fine for finishing quilts with straight edges.

Binding cut from the *crosswise* grain has a bit of stretch. Although it may require piecing to get the desired length, binding cut from the crosswise grain is my personal preference. It often requires that you purchase less fabric, and—since strips cut crosswise are often slightly off-grain—minimizes the chance that

any one single thread runs the entire folded edge of the binding, making it more vulnerable to wear.

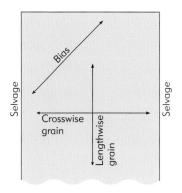

Binding cut on the true diagonal—or *bias*—of the fabric, is excellent for finishing curved edges. Because it has a fair amount of stretch, bias binding eases comfortably around curves. In addition, binding cut on the bias tends to wear better since it is cut *across*, rather than along, the weave of the fabric.

Because it tends to stretch, take extra care with bias binding. Handle it gently and use lots of pins to avoid getting ripples in the finished edge.

> Striped fabrics create interesting effects when cut on the bias, making them a great choice for bias binding.

Figuring Binding Length

To figure how much binding you'll need, measure around the outside edges of your quilt top, and add at least 12″ for seams, starting and finishing, and turning corners.

To figure how much binding you'll need for a quilt with curved (*e.g.*, scalloped) edges, run a length of string around the outside edges and add at least 12″ for seams, starting, and ending.

When you need to piece strips to get the necessary length of binding, piece them with a diagonal seam, as described for borders on page 8. Press seams open to prevent lumps in the binding, and match thread color to the binding fabric to keep seams less noticeable.

> Add an interesting design element to pieced binding by using a variety of different fabrics from the quilt. The binding on *Irish Nine-Patch* (page 36) is a good example.

Double-Fold Binding

Double-fold binding, also called French-fold binding, is what I use for my quilts. The double thickness makes it extra sturdy—perfect for a quilt destined for lots of use. You can double-fold both straight-grain and bias binding.

To figure how wide to cut the binding strips, multiply the finished width of the binding by 4. Add ½″ for seam allowances, and an additional ⅛″ to turn over the edge of the batting.

Since I prefer the look of a narrow ⅜″-wide binding, I typically cut double-fold binding strips 2⅛″ wide (⅜″ × 4 = 1½″ + ½″ = 2″ + ⅛″ = 2⅛″).

1. Figure the length of binding you need as described in the previous section. Cut strips to the desired width.

2. Piece the strips end to end with diagonal seams.

3. Fold and press lengthwise, right sides out.

> Store prepared binding on an empty paper towel roll to keep it neat and tangle-free until you need it.

Preparing the Quilt for Binding

The binding on your quilt should be firm and filled with batting. This looks better, and is better for the life of the binding.

1. Use your rotary cutter and ruler to straighten the sides and square the corners of your quilt as needed before you add the binding. Be careful not to trim off any important block elements (such as points) in the process.

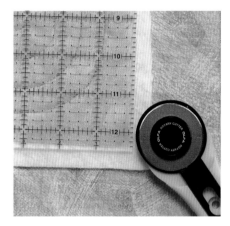

For ⅜″-wide binding, trim the edges of the batting and backing ⅛″ beyond the raw edge of the quilt top. When you align the raw edge of the binding with the raw edge of the quilt top, and sew it to the quilt with a ¼″ seam, the binding will be perfectly filled. If you do not have a ¼″ presser foot, adjust the needle position or use masking tape on the throat plate for a ⅜″ seam allowance.

2. Machine baste with a large stitch around the perimeter of the quilt top, approximately ⅛″–³⁄₁₆″ inside the raw edge. This secures the three layers as you sew the binding to the quilt.

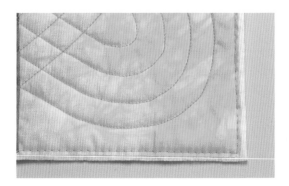

Squared Corners

Individual binding strips added separately to each side of your quilt is the easiest of all binding treatments. The binding ends are neatly squared, so you don't need to worry about turning corners. *Rail Fence* (page 26) features this finishing.

1. Prepare the quilt for binding by trimming the batting and backing as described on page 16.

2. Measure the quilt from top to bottom as described on page 7. Refer to Double-Fold Binding (page 16) to cut and prepare two binding strips the length of the quilt + 1".

3. Align the raw edges of a binding strip with the raw edges of one side (left or right) of the quilt top, allowing the strip to extend ½" past each corner. Sew the strip to the quilt with a ¼" seam. Repeat for the opposite side of the quilt.

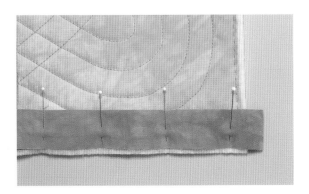

4. Bring the folded edge of the binding over the raw edges to the quilt back, covering the seamline. Use matching-colored thread and small stitches to slipstitch the binding securely to the quilt back. Trim the ends of the binding even with the quilt.

5. Measure the quilt from side to side, including the binding. Cut two binding strips the width of the quilt + 1". Fold and press as before, turning under the two ends ½" to create a finished edge.

6. Align the raw edges of a binding strip with the raw edges of the top and bottom edges of the quilt top, and the turned-under ends with the corners of the quilt. Sew the binding to the quilt.

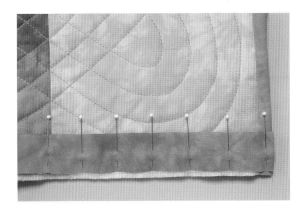

7. Bring the folded edge of the binding to the quilt back and slipstitch in place, using a thread color that matches the binding. Remember to also stitch the ends closed.

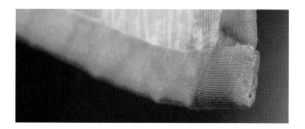

Mitered Corners

Bindings with mitered corners are my personal favorites, so it's not surprising I used them on three projects in this book (*Amish Baskets* on page 29, *Unknown Star* on page 33, and *Scrappy Triangles* on page 44). Miters aren't difficult, and I like the polished look they give.

Two different methods are presented for starting and ending the binding: the fold-and-tuck method appears here, and the seamed method appears on pages 19–20.

1. Refer to page 7 to measure, and page 16 to prepare the quilt.

2. Open and trim the starting end of the binding at a 45° angle and press under a ¼″ seam allowance. Refold the binding.

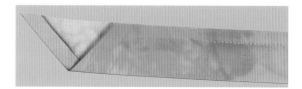

3. Beginning at least 12″ from a corner, align the raw edge of the binding with the raw edge of the quilt top. Pin up to the first corner.

4. Leave the first few inches of binding free, and stitch the binding to the quilt with a ¼″ seam. Stop and backstitch ¼″ from the first corner.

5. Lift the presser foot and needle, and rotate the quilt one-quarter turn to the left. Fold the binding strip so it forms a 45° angle and extends straight above the quilt, its raw edge even with the raw edge of the quilt top.

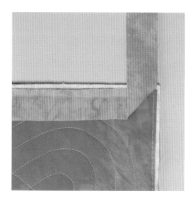

6. Fold the binding strip straight down, aligning its raw edge with the edge of the quilt top. Resume stitching at the folded edge.

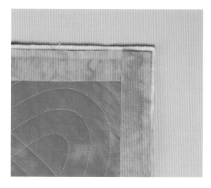

7. Continue pinning and stitching the binding to the quilt, turning each corner as described in Steps 4–6. As you approach the starting point,

stop and trim the end of the binding so it overlaps the start by about 3″.

8. Tuck the trimmed end of the binding inside the folded end, making sure the join is smooth. Pin and finish stitching the binding to the quilt.

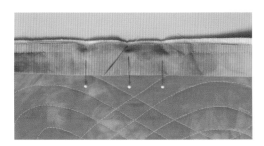

9. Bring the folded edge of the binding over the raw edges to the quilt back, covering the seamline. Use matching-colored thread and small stitches to slipstitch the binding securely to the quilt back. A miter will form naturally at each corner. Stitch both the front and back folded miter closed with an invisible (blind) stitch.

Seamed Method to End Binding

This method of binding finishes with a seam, rather than by tucking one end inside the other. The join is less obvious since there is less bulk.

1. Prepare the quilt and binding as usual. Do not angle or turn under the end of the binding.

2. Beginning near the center of one side of the quilt, align the raw edge of the binding with the raw edge of the quilt top. Leaving approximately 12″ free, pin up to the first corner.

3. Sew the binding to the quilt as described in Mitered Corners, Steps 3–6 (page 18). Stop approximately 10″–15″ from where you started stitching the binding to the quilt. Take the quilt from the machine, placing it on a flat surface, such as your ironing board or cutting mat.

4. Lay the ending tail of the binding strip over the unstitched starting tail, aligning the raw edges of both strips with the quilt top. Crease the ending tail, or mark it with a pencil, at the point it meets the start. Measure the *cut* width of the binding strip from the crease (or pencil mark). Cut the ending tail at this point.

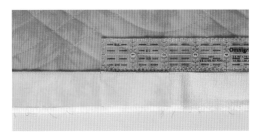

5. Open both tails and place them right sides together at a 90° angle. Mark a diagonal seam, pin, then stitch with matching-colored thread.

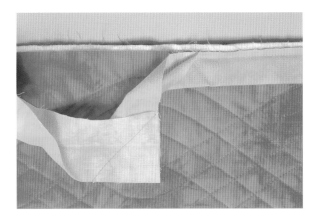

6. Trim the excess binding to a ¼″ seam allowance, and press the seam open. Refold the binding strip, and finish stitching it to the quilt.

Scalloped-Edge Binding

Scalloped edges, as in *Irish Nine-Patch* on page 36, require a bias binding that will ease around the curves. Cut individual bias strips and piece together using diagonal seams (page 8).

1. Machine baste a scant ¼" inside the marked scallop. Trim the layers along the marked scallop line.

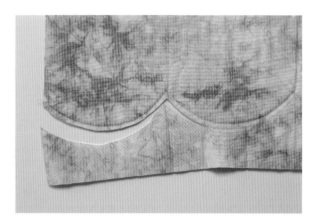

2. Make a mark ¼" inside each dent. Clip the raw edge at each dent, stopping just before the mark and basting stitches.

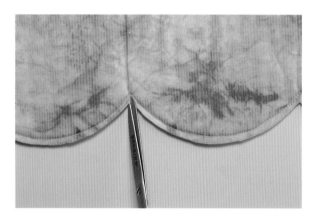

3. Prepare double-fold binding as described on page 16. Press the seams open. (I started and ended the binding with the seamed method described on page 19.)

4. Working from the front, begin pinning the binding to the quilt, aligning the raw edge of the binding to the raw edge of the quilt top. Start on the side of a scallop, rather than on the center of a scallop or in a dent, and place the pins perpendicular to the edge of the quilt. (They'll be easier to remove as you stitch.) Be careful not to stretch the binding. Instead, ease it gently around the curve.

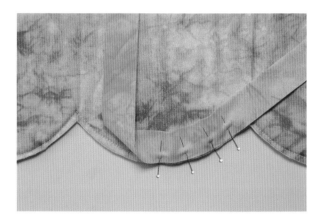

5. When you reach the first dent, spread the scallops to form a straight line. Continue pinning the binding to this "straight" edge, placing a pin on either side of the dent to keep the binding aligned. Continue your way around the quilt, pinning the binding to each scallop and dent.

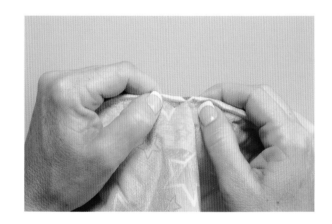

6. Working from the back, stitch the binding to the quilt with a ¼″ seam. Remove each pin as you reach it. Stitch each dent just as you pinned it—by gently separating the scallops to sew a straight line. Make sure to stay on the inside of the clip.

7. Beginning along the side of a scallop, turn the binding over the raw edge of the quilt and use matching-colored thread and an invisible stitch to secure the binding to the quilt back. Work one scallop at a time; stop just before you reach the first dent.

8. Make a fold and carefully coax the binding to the back of the quilt. Cover the seamline, match the fold to the point of the dent, and continue stitching. The result is a nice, soft miter.

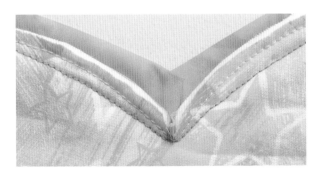

I used random-length strips for the pieced bias binding on *Irish Nine-Patch* (page 36). As a result, I didn't have to worry about seams in awkward places. If I needed to, I could simply adjust the length of the troublesome strip—no math!

■ Folded Piping

Amish Baskets (page 29) features a narrow, folded piping (no cording inside) inserted between its outermost border and mitered binding. This accent acts like a double mat on a nicely framed picture, adding a flash of color and a touch of elegance.

To figure how wide to cut the piping, multiply the desired finished width of the piping by 2, and add ½″ for seam allowances.

For quilts with straight sides, cut piping strips from the straight grain of the fabric. For quilts with curved edges, cut strips on the bias. You can cut strips on the bias for design purposes as well.

1. Prepare the quilt for binding by trimming the batting and backing as described on page 16.

2. Measure the quilt as described on page 7. Add 2″–3″ to both the length and width, and cut 2 strips to each measurement, piecing them if necessary. Press the seams open. Fold the strips lengthwise, right side out, and press.

3. Pin the piping strips to the appropriate sides of the quilt, aligning the raw edges with the raw edges of the quilt top. The strips should overlap and extend beyond each corner by 1″–1½″. Baste the strips to the quilt with a ⅛″ seam.

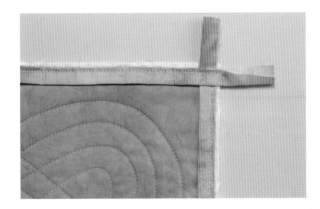

4. Align the raw edge of the binding with the raw edge of the piping and quilt top. Stitch the binding to the quilt with your chosen technique. Trim the excess ends of the piping strips.

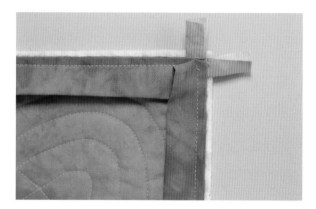

5. Turn the binding to the quilt back and finish as described on page 19. Turn your quilt over and admire your piping!

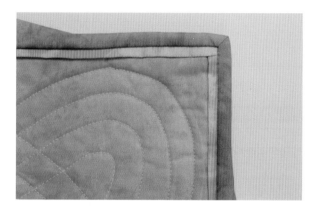

If your quilt features piecing in the outermost border (e.g., the Cake Stand corner blocks in *Amish Baskets*), you may need to make *slight* adjustments so the piping doesn't cover any points. Before trimming the backing and batting, position the piping as you wish it to appear on the finished quilt. Baste the piping in place, and trim the batting and backing to the piping's raw edge. (For *Amish Baskets*, the batting and backing were trimmed approximately 1/8" beyond the quilt top.) Align the binding with the raw edges of the piping, batting, and backing, and stitch with a *generous* 1/4" seam.

Prairie Points

Prairie points are triangles made from folded squares of fabric, adding dimension to the edges of your quilt. Unlike bindings, which cover the outside edges of the quilt, prairie points are inserted *between* the layers. They are stitched to the quilt top before it is layered and quilted.

It's important to keep the size of the prairie points in proportion to the rest of the quilt. If you are unsure which size to use, cut, fold, and audition triangles of various sizes. Experiment with fabrics, too: depending upon the quilt, cut them all from a single fabric, choose two or three fabrics from your quilt, or—for a scrappy quilt—go totally scrappy.

The length (long, raw edge) of the prairie point equals the side of the cut square. You'll overlap the prairie points, so you'll need extras to cover the measurements of your quilt.

1. Fold each square on the diagonal, right side out; press. Then, fold in half along its folded side; press.

2. Fold the quilt top in half in both directions and crease lightly to identify the midpoint on each side.

3. With right sides together and raw edges aligned, place prairie points along one side of the quilt top. Place a prairie point centered over the midpoint first, then one at each end. Be sure the openings in all prairie points face the same direction.

4. Fill the side with additional prairie points. Slip the folded edge of each new point inside the open end of its neighbor, overlapping as needed to evenly fill the space. (You can use elements in the quilt top as guides for spacing prairie points.) When you are satisfied with the placement, secure each prairie point with a single pin perpendicular to the raw edge.

5. Repeat Steps 3–4 for the remaining sides of the quilt top. Make sure the number of prairie points on the top and bottom match. And, make sure the number of prarie points on the sides match.

6. Sew the prairie points to the quilt with a ¼″ seam, pivoting at the corners. Remove the pins as you go.

7. Layer, baste, and quilt the quilt top. Stop quilting approximately ½″ from the edge.

8. Trim the backing ¼″ beyond the raw edges of the quilt top and prairie points. Carefully trim *only the batting* slightly less than the raw edge of the quilt top and prairie points.

9. Turn (or press) the prairie points away from the center of the quilt. (The seam allowance will turn inward.) Wrap the backing over the edge of the batting. Secure the backing to the prairie points with pins or basting, then hand stitch with color-matched thread and an invisible stitch.

10. If you wish, finish with a line of quilting ¼″ from the folded edge, all around the perimeter of the quilt.

General Quiltmaking Basics

■ Pinning

Careful pinning helps ease a finicky border to fit. It also keeps raw edges from drifting apart as you stitch, a real plus when sewing long seams to add borders or bindings.

■ Piecing

Unless instructed otherwise, use a ¼″ seam allowance throughout.

■ Pressing

Whenever possible, press seams in opposite directions. Pressing arrows are included to help you.

I press pieced units and blocks *right* side up on a *firm* surface to avoid pressing tucks in the seams. I press appliqué *wrong* side up on a thick, *soft* surface so the appliqué shapes keep their "dimension."

■ Sets

The projects feature two different block arrangements (sets): the straight set and the diagonal set.

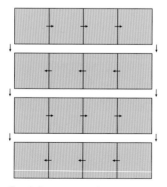

Straight set pressing

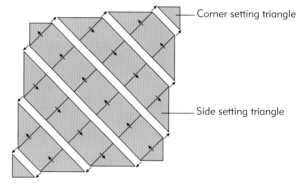

Diagonal set pressing

Cut setting triangles so the straight grain falls along the outside edge of the quilt top. This means cutting the large side setting triangles as quarter-square triangles, and the smaller corner triangles as half-square triangles. (I've included a chart below to help you cut squares for setting triangles for future quilts.) Be careful the iron doesn't touch any exposed bias when you press setting triangles.

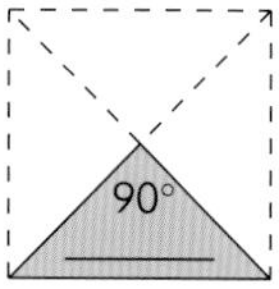

Side setting (quarter-square) triangle. Grainline is indicated.

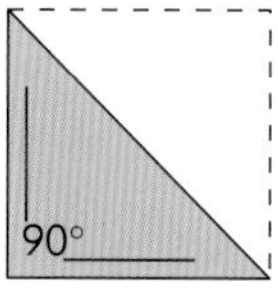

Corner setting (half-square) triangle. Grainline is indicated.

Finished block size	Half-square triangle	Quarter-square triangle
4½″	4⅛″ square	7⅝″ square
6″	5⅛″ square	9¾″ square
8″	6⅝″ square	12⅝″ square
9″	7¼″ square	14″ square
10″	8″ square	15½″ square
12″	9⅜″ square	18¼″ square

Backing

If your quilt top is wider than the standard 42"-wide cotton fabric, you will need to piece the backing. Yardages given in the project instructions include at least 2" extra all around the outside of the quilt top. (The same is true for the batting.)

Layering and Basting

Spread the backing wrong side up on your (non-loop) carpet or work surface. Smooth the backing, and secure it with T-pins or masking tape. Center the batting on top of the backing, and trim the two layers so the raw edges match. Center the quilt top right side up onto the batting and smooth out the wrinkles.

For hand quilting, baste the three layers together in a 4" grid pattern. For machine quilting, secure the three layers every 3" with rustproof, size #1 safety pins. In either case, baste all the way to the edges of the quilt top.

Quilting

Refer to the project quilts for quilt design inspiration.

Hanging Sleeve

1. Cut a strip of fabric the width of the quilt × 8" wide. Hem each of the short edges. Fold the strip in half lengthwise, wrong sides together and stitch. Press seam open.

2. Position the sleeve with the long seam against the back of the quilt. Pin and whip stitch the long folded edges to the back of the quilt.

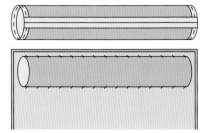

Quilt Labels

The information you include on your label will be treasured for generations to come. Use a permanent fabric pen on the back (or even on the front) of the quilt or a beautiful patch, designed specifically for the quilt with embroidery or colorful fabric pens. Before sewing the label onto the back, consider also writing directly on the quilt (where the label will cover) for assurance that any information will not be lost in the event the label is taken off.

Always include:

1. Name of the maker and the quilter (if different)

2. Date

3. Where the quilt was made

Optional but a wonderful addition:

4. For whom the quilt was made and the associated event

5. Any personal sentiments

6. Ribbons or prizes the quilt has won

We used an antique quilt I own as an example on my television show *Simply Quilts*. The quilt included the name of the maker, the town in which it was made, and a date. My guest, Nancy Kirk, was very impressed with the age of the quilt. It was one of the earliest red and green quilts she had ever seen, which provided information about the value of the quilt. In addition, a viewer from the area where the quilt was made saw the show and wrote to me with the family history of a quilt. Now, 150 years later, I am grateful that a quilter took the time to provide clues to the origins of this masterpiece.

Rail Fence

You can strip piece the quilt in a limited scrappy palette as described in the following instructions, or piece the strips individually in a totally scrappy palette as shown in the photograph. Surround the lighter blocks in the center of the quilt with the darker blocks for a simple self-border.

This Rail Fence variation measures approximately 47 1⁄8" × 55", and includes seventy-two 5 1⁄2" pieced blocks set on point.

■ Fabric Requirements

Fabric amounts are based on a 42″ fabric width.

Assorted white, cream, and light tan prints:
⅓ yard each of 5 different fabrics for Rail Fence blocks

Assorted dark red, navy, and brown prints:
⅓ yard each of 7 different fabrics for Rail Fence blocks

Assorted medium tan and brown prints: ⅓ yard each of 2 different fabrics for Rail Fence blocks

Assorted medium-dark and dark tan and brown prints: ⅝ yard total for side and corner triangles

Dark red print: ½ yard for binding

Batting: 51″ × 59″

Backing: 3 yards

■ Cutting

Assorted white, cream, and light tan prints

Cut a total of 36 strips 1 ¼″ × the fabric width (in matching sets of 4) for the Rail Fence blocks.

Assorted dark red, navy, and brown prints

Cut a total of 45 strips 1″ × the fabric width (in matching sets of 5) for the Rail Fence blocks.

Cut a total of 16 strips 1 ¼″ × the fabric width (in matching sets of 4) for the Rail Fence blocks.

Assorted medium tan and brown prints

Cut a total of 20 strips 1″ × the fabric width (in matching sets of 5) for the Rail Fence blocks.

Assorted medium-dark and dark tan and brown prints

Cut a total of 6 squares 9 ⅛″ × 9 ⅛″, then cut twice diagonally. You'll need 22 for the side triangles.

Cut a total of 2 squares 4 ⅞″ × 4 ⅞″, then cut in half diagonally. You'll need 4 for the corner triangles.

Dark red print

Cut 6 strips 2 ⅛″ × the fabric width for the binding.

■ Piecing and Pressing

Use ¼″ seam allowances. Press in the direction of the arrows.

Rail Fence Blocks

You'll need a total of 72 Rail Fence blocks: 50 Block A and 22 Block B.

1. Arrange 4 matching 1¼″-wide white, cream, or light tan print strips and 5 matching 1″-wide dark red, navy, or brown print strips, alternating them as shown. Stitch the strips together; press. Make 9 strip sets.

2. Cut into 6″ segments for 50 Block A.

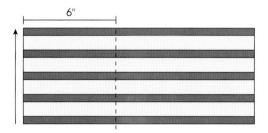

3. Arrange 4 matching 1¼″-wide dark red, navy, and brown print strips and 5 matching medium tan and brown 1″-wide print strips, alternating them as shown. Stitch the strips together; press. Make 4 strip sets.

4. Cut into 6″ segments for 22 Block B.

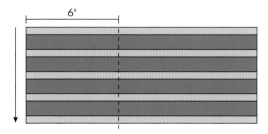

■ Quilt Top Assembly

1. Lay out the Rail Fence blocks on point, turning them as shown in the quilt construction diagram

below. Place A blocks in the center of the quilt, and B blocks around the outside edges. Finish with the medium-dark and dark tan and brown print side and corner triangles.

2. Stitch the blocks, side, and corner triangles in diagonal rows; press.

3. Stitch the rows together; press. Your quilt top should measure approximately 47 ⅛″ × 55″.

■ Quilting and Finishing

1. Layer, baste, and quilt your quilt top.

2. Refer to Double-Fold Binding (page 16) and stitch the 2 ⅛″-wide dark red print strips end to end, with diagonal seams as described on page 8.

3. Refer to Squared Corners (pages 17–18) and stitch the binding to the quilt.

Amish Baskets

A series of borders in varying sizes and corner squares create visual interest. The Cake Stand blocks are simpler "cousins" of the center block, and help to unify the overall design. A narrow, folded piping adds pizzazz to the straightforward mitered binding.

This medallion-style wallhanging is 38½" × 38½" and features a single 12" Basket block set on point. A 6" variation called Cake Stand finishes each corner of the outer border.

Fabric Requirements

Fabric amounts are based on a 42″ fabric width.

Yellow check: ¼ yard for Basket block

Assorted rosy-red prints: ⅓ yard total for Basket and Cake Stand blocks

Assorted yellow prints: ⅛ yard total for Basket block

Yellow and rosy-red small print: ⅓ yard for Basket block and corner squares

Yellow and rosy-red large-scale print: 1 ¼ yards for setting triangles and outer border

Red check: ⅓ yard for inner border and folded piping

Rosy-red tone-on-tone print: ¾ yard for middle border, Cake Stand blocks, and binding*

Yellow print: ¼ yard for Cake Stand blocks

Batting: 42″ × 42″

Backing: 1 ¼ yards

* You can use leftover scraps for Basket block.

Cutting

Yellow check

Cut 1 square 4⅞″ × 4⅞″, then cut in half diagonally. You'll need 1 triangle for the Basket block (E).

Cut 4 squares 2⅞″ × 2⅞″, then cut in half diagonally. You'll need 8 triangles for the Basket block (A).

Cut 2 strips 2½″ × 8½″ for the Basket block (D).

Cut 1 square 2½″ × 2½″ for the Basket block (B).

Assorted rosy-red prints

Cut a total of 10 squares 2⅞″ × 2⅞″, then cut in half diagonally. You'll need 20 triangles for the Basket block (A).

Cut a total of 2 squares 3⅞″ × 3⅞″, then cut in half diagonally. You'll need 4 triangles for the Cake Stand blocks (I).

Assorted yellow prints

Cut 3 squares 2⅞″ × 2⅞″, then cut in half diagonally. You'll need 6 triangles for the Basket block (A).

Yellow and rosy-red small print

Cut 1 square 8⅞″ × 8⅞″, then cut in half diagonally. You'll need 1 triangle for the Basket block (C).

Cut 4 squares 2″ × 2″ for the corner squares.

Cut 4 squares 3½″ × 3½″ for the corner squares.

Yellow and rosy-red large-scale print

Cut 2 squares 9⅜″ × 9⅜″, then cut in half diagonally. You'll need 4 for the setting triangles (F).

Cut 4 strips 6½″ × the fabric width for the outer border.

Red check

Cut 2 strips 2″ × the fabric width for the inner border. Cut each strip in half.

Cut 4 strips 1″ × the fabric width for the piping.

Rosy-red tone-on-tone print

Cut 2 strips 3 ½″ × the fabric width for the middle border. Cut each strip in half.

Cut 4 strips 2 ⅛″ × the fabric width for the binding.

Cut 2 squares 3 ⅞″ × 3 ⅞″, then cut in half diagonally. You'll need 4 triangles for the Cake Stand blocks (I).

Cut 8 squares 2 ⅜″ × 2 ⅜″, then cut in half diagonally. You'll need 16 triangles for the Cake Stand blocks (G).

Cut 1 strip 2″ × the fabric width, then cut into 8 strips 2″ × 3 ½″ (J) and 4 squares 2″ × 2″ (H) for the Cake Stand blocks.

Yellow print

Cut 2 squares 3⅞″ × 3⅞″, then cut in half diagonally. You'll need 4 triangles for the Cake Stand blocks (I).

Cut 12 squares 2⅜″ × 2⅜″, then cut in half diagonally. You'll need 24 triangles for the Cake Stand blocks (G).

Piecing and Pressing

Use ¼″ seam allowances. Press in the direction of the arrows.

Basket Block

1. Stitch yellow check and assorted rosy-red print A triangles in pairs; press. Make 8. Stitch in groups of 4 as shown; press. Make 1 of each.

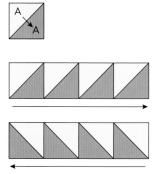

Stitch in pairs, then stitch in groups of 4.

2. Stitch assorted yellow print and rosy-red print A triangles in pairs; press. Make 6. Arrange with assorted rosy-red print A triangles in rows as shown. Stitch the units and triangles into rows; press. Stitch the rows together; press.

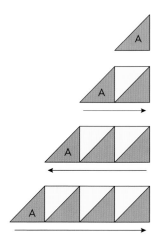

Stitch the units and triangles into rows, then stitch the rows together.

3. Stitch yellow check strips to rosy-red print A triangles as shown; press. Make 1 of each.

Stitch strips and triangles.

4. Arrange the units from Steps 1–3, and C triangle, the 2½" yellow check B square and E triangle as shown. Sew the block together; press.

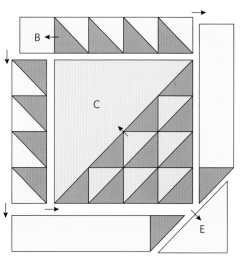

Sew the block together.

5. Stitch a yellow and rosy-red print F triangle to each side of the Basket block; press. The block should now measure approximately 17½" × 17½".

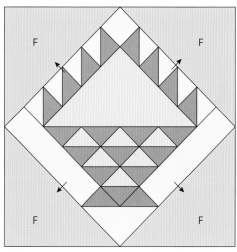

Stitch triangles to Basket block.

Cake Stand Blocks

1. Stitch yellow print and rosy-red tone-on-tone print G triangles in pairs; press. Make 16. Stitch pairs together as shown on the next page; press. Make 4 of each direction.

2. Stitch yellow print and assorted rosy-red print I triangles in pairs; press. Make 4.

3. Stitch rosy-red tone-on-tone print J strips to yellow print G triangles as shown; press. Make 4 of each direction.

4. Arrange the units from Steps 1–3, and the 2″ rosy-red tone-on-tone H square and I/I unit as shown. Sew the block together; press. Make 4. The block should measure 6½″ × 6½″.

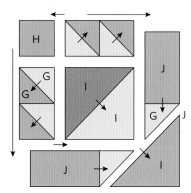

Sew the block together.

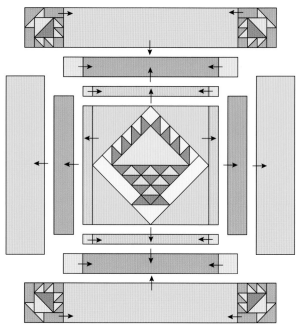

Quilt construction

■ Quilt Top Assembly

1. Lay out the Basket block, the 2″ yellow and rosy-red print corner squares, and the red check inner borders as shown in the quilt construction diagram. Refer to Borders with Corner Squares (page 12) and stitch the inner border to the quilt. Press.

2. Repeat Step 1 to stitch the 3½″ yellow and rosy-red print corner squares and the rosy-red tone-on-tone print middle borders to the quilt; press. Add the yellow and rosy-red large-scale print outer borders, positioning the Cake Stand corner blocks as shown in the quilt construction diagram. Press.

■ Quilting and Finishing

1. Layer, baste, and quilt your quilt top.

2. Use the 1″-wide red check strips to make piping as described in Folded Piping (pages 21–22).

3. Refer to Double-Fold Binding (page 16), and stitch the 2⅛″-wide rosy-red tone-on-tone print strips end to end, with diagonal seams as described on page 8.

4. Refer to Folded Piping (pages 21–22) and Mitered Corners (pages 18–19) and stitch the piping and binding to the quilt, mitering the binding corners.

A pieced Sawtooth border repeats and complements the triangle shapes in the block. You can work in a scrappy palette as described in the following instructions, in a more limited scrappy palette as shown in the photograph, or in a simple, two-fabric palette of blue and white.

This crisp blue and white quilt measures 63½″ × 63½″, and features nine 18″ Star blocks in a straight set.

▥ Fabric Requirements

Fabric amounts are based on a 42″ fabric width.

Assorted white-with-blue prints: 3½ yards total for Star blocks and Sawtooth border

Assorted blue prints: 2¼ yards total for Star blocks, Sawtooth border, and pieced binding

Narrow blue-and-white stripe: ½ yard for inner border

Batting: 68″ × 68″

Backing: 3⅞ yards

▥ Cutting

Assorted white-with-blue prints

Cut a total of 3 strips 10¼″ × the fabric width. Cut into 9 squares 10¼″ × 10¼″, then cut twice diagonally. You'll need 36 triangles for the Star blocks (B).

Cut a total of 3 strips 5⅜″ × the fabric width. Cut into 18 squares 5⅜″ × 5⅜″, then cut in half diagonally. You'll need 36 triangles for the Star blocks (C).

Cut a total of 5 strips 5″ × the fabric width, then cut into 36 squares 5″ × 5″ for the Star blocks (D).

Cut a total of 5 strips 3⅛″ × the fabric width. Cut into 54 squares 3⅛″ × 3⅛″, then cut in half diagonally. You'll need 108 for the Star blocks (A).

Cut a total of 4 strips 3⅞″ × the fabric width. Cut into 38 squares 3⅞″ × 3⅞″, then cut in half diagonally. You'll need 76 triangles for the Sawtooth border (E).

Cut a total of 4 squares 3½″ × 3½″ for the Sawtooth border (F).

Assorted blue prints

Cut a total of 14 strips 3⅛″ × the fabric width. Cut into 162 squares 3⅛″ × 3⅛″, then cut each square in half diagonally. You'll need 324 triangles for the Star blocks (A).

Cut a total of 4 strips 3⅞″ × the fabric width. Cut into 38 squares 3⅞″ × 3⅞″, then cut each square in half diagonally. You'll need 76 triangles for the Sawtooth border (E).

Cut a total of 7 strips 2⅛″ × the fabric width for the pieced binding.

Narrow blue-and-white stripe

Cut 6 strips 2″ × the fabric width for the inner border.

▥ Piecing and Pressing

Use ¼″ seam allowances. Press in the direction of the arrows.

Star Blocks

1. Stitch assorted white-with-blue and blue print A triangles in pairs; press. Make 108.

2. Stitch blue print A triangles to each unit from Step 1 as shown; press. Make 108.

3. Stitch 2 units from Step 2 to a white-with-blue print B triangle; press. Make 36.

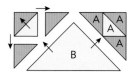

Stitch units to B triangles.

4. Stitch a remaining unit from Step 2 to a white-with-blue print C triangle; press. Make 36.

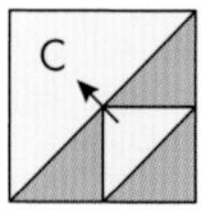

Stitch units to C triangles.

5. Stitch 4 units from Step 4 together as shown; press. Make 9.

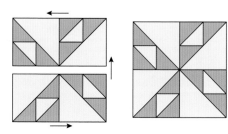

Stitch units as shown.

6. Arrange 4 white-with-blue print D squares, 4 units from Step 3, and a unit from Step 5 in 3 rows as shown. Stitch the squares and units into rows; press. Stitch the rows together; press. Make 9.

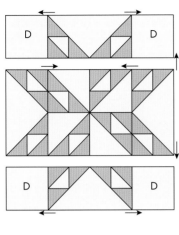

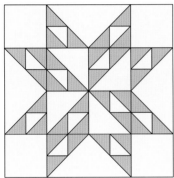

Stitch as shown.

Sawtooth Border

1. Stitch white-with-blue print and blue print E triangles in pairs; press. Make 76.

Stitch triangles in pairs.

2. Refer to the quilt construction diagram and use the units from Step 1 to stitch 4 borders of 19 units each. Change the direction of the triangles in each border as shown.

▦ Quilt Top Assembly

1. Lay out the 9 Star blocks as shown.

2. Stitch the blocks into rows; press.

3. Stitch the rows together; press. Your quilt top should measure 54½" × 54½".

4. Join the 2"-wide stripe strips end to end. Refer to Partial-Seam Borders (pages 11–12) to trim and sew the inner borders to the quilt top.

5. Refer to Borders with Corner Squares (page 12) and stitch the Sawtooth borders to the quilt, adding the F white-with-blue print corner squares.

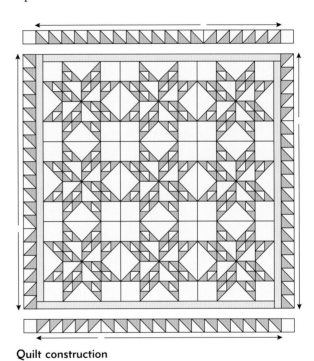

Quilt construction

▦ Quilting and Finishing

1. Layer, baste, and quilt your quilt top.

2. Refer to Double-Fold Binding (page 16) and stitch the 2⅛"-wide assorted blue print strips end to end, with diagonal the seams as described on page 8.

3. Refer to Mitered Corners (pages 18–19) and stitch the binding to the quilt.

Irish Nine-Patch

Borders can take on "wow" appeal with the addition of fabulous quilting designs. The quilting template dictated the size and scale of the scallop, and the wonderful machine quilting brought the design to life. I finished the curvy edges with a scrappy pieced bias binding.

This Irish Chain and Nine-Patch variation is 74½" × 88" and is made up of twenty 13½" Double Nine-Patch blocks.

◼ Fabric Requirements

Fabric amounts are based on a 42″ fabric width.

Off-white print: 4¾ yards for nine-patch units, alternate squares, and outer border

White solid: 1 yard for nine-patch units

Black print: ⅓ yard for nine-patch units

Assorted bright prints: 1⅝ yards total for nine-patch units and pieced binding

Lime-green print: ½ yard for inner border

Batting: 79″ × 92″

Backing: 5¼ yards

◼ Cutting

Off-white print

Cut 9 strips 9 ½″ × the fabric width for the outer border.

Cut 10 strips 5″ × the fabric width, then cut into 80 squares 5″ × 5″ for the alternate squares.

Cut 12 strips 2″ × the fabric width, then cut into 240 squares 2″ × 2″ for the nine-patch units.

White solid

Cut 16 strips 2″ × the fabric width, then cut into 320 squares 2″ × 2″ for the nine-patch units.

Black print

Cut 4 strips 2″ × the fabric width, then cut into 80 squares 2″ × 2″ for the nine-patch units.

Assorted bright prints

Cut strips 2″ × the fabric width, then cut into a total of 260 squares 2″ × 2″ for the nine-patch units. Set the remaining fabric aside for the pieced bias binding.

Lime-green print

Cut 9 strips 1 ½″ × the fabric width for the inner border.

◼ Piecing and Pressing

Use ¼″ seam allowances. Press in the direction of the arrows.

Nine-Patch Units

You'll need a total of 100 nine-patch units for the Double Nine-Patch blocks: 20 each of Units 1–5.

1. Arrange 4 white solid 2″ squares and 5 assorted bright print 2″ squares in 3 rows as shown. Stitch the squares into rows; press. Stitch the rows together; press. Make 20.

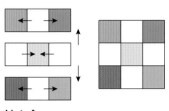

Unit 1

2. Arrange 3 white solid 2″ squares, 2 assorted bright print 2″ squares, 3 off-white print squares, and 1 black print square in 3 rows as shown. Stitch the squares into rows; press. Stitch the rows together; press. Make 20.

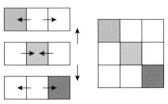

Unit 2

3. Repeat the instructions for nine-patch Unit 2, arranging the 2″ squares as shown for Units 3, 4, and 5. Make 20 each. Note the placement of white solid and off-white print squares differ in each unit.

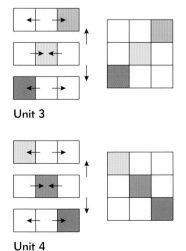

Unit 3

Unit 4

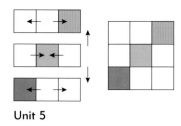

Unit 5

Double Nine-Patch Blocks

You'll need 10 each of Block A and Block B.

1. Arrange 1 nine-patch Unit 1, 2 each of nine-patch Unit 2 and Unit 3, and 4 off-white print 5″ squares in 3 rows as shown. Stitch the units and squares into rows; press. Stitch the rows together; press. Make 10.

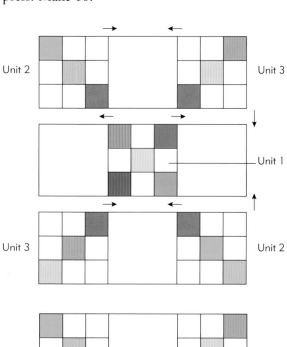

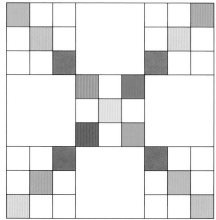

Block A

2. Arrange 1 nine-patch Unit 1, 2 each of nine-patch Unit 4 and Unit 5, and 4 off-white print 5″ squares in 3 rows as shown. Repeat Step 1 to assemble the block. Make 10.

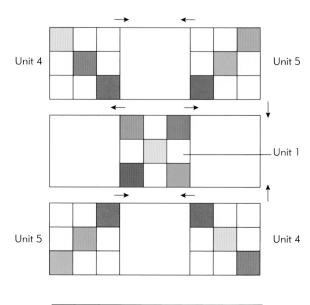

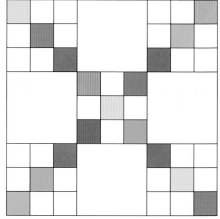

Block B

■ Quilt Top Assembly

1. Lay out the 20 Double Nine-Patch blocks, alternating Block A and Block B as shown in the quilt construction diagram.

2. Stitch the blocks into rows; press.

3. Stitch the rows together; press. Your quilt top should measure 54½″ × 68″.

Quilt construction

■ Adding the Borders

1. Join the 1½″-wide lime-green print strips end to end. Trim to make 2 strips 77″ long for the top and bottom borders and 2 strips 90″ long for the side borders.

2. Repeat Step 1, using the 9½″-wide off-white print strips.

3. Stitch lime-green and off-white strips of matching length together side by side to make 4 border units.

4. Refer to Mitered Borders (pages 9–10) and stitch the 77″-long border units to the top and bottom, and the 90″-long border units to the sides of the quilt top.

5. Refer to Scalloped Borders (pages 13–14) to decide when to mark the scalloped edge on the outside border.

■ Quilting and Finishing

1. Layer, baste, and quilt your quilt top.

2. Cut the remaining assorted bright-colored prints into 2⅛″-wide bias strips of random length. Refer to Double-Fold Binding (page 16) and stitch the strips together into a 350″ length of scrappy binding, angling the seams as described on page 8.

3. Refer to Scalloped-Edge Binding (pages 20–21) and stitch the binding to the quilt.

Butterfly

The scrappy pastel palette and whimsical retro design of this quilt called out for a playful finish. I think you'll agree: prairie points are perfect! Fuse web and finish the butterflies with a machine blanket stitch or add a turn-under allowance and hand appliqué the bodies.

This quilt measures approximately 44½" × 51" plus the prairie points, and alternates fifty-six 4½" Butterfly blocks with forty-two 4½" Snowball blocks—all set on point.

■ Fabric Requirements

Fabric amounts are based on a 42″ fabric width.

Off-white muslin: 2½ yards for Butterfly blocks, Snowball blocks, and side and corner triangles

Assorted 1930s-style pastel prints: 1¼ yards total for Butterfly blocks

Assorted pastel solids: ⅝ yard total for Snowball blocks

Black solid: ¼ yard for side triangles*

Assorted 1930s-style blue prints and solids: 1¼ yards total for prairie points

Batting: 49″ × 55″

Backing: 2¾ yards

Fusible web (optional): ½ yard for Butterfly blocks

Black embroidery floss: for Butterfly blocks

* You can use leftover scraps for Snowball blocks.

■ Cutting

Off-white muslin

Cut 2 strips 7⅝″ × the fabric width. Cut into 7 squares 7⅝″ × 7⅝″, then cut twice diagonally. You'll need 26 for the side triangles (F). (You'll have 2 triangles left over.)

Cut 2 squares 4⅛″ × 4⅛″, then cut in half diagonally. You'll need 4 for the corner triangles (G).

Cut 6 strips 5″ × the fabric width, then cut into 42 squares 5″ × 5″ for the Snowball blocks (D).

Cut 4 strips 2⅜″ × the fabric width. Cut into 56 squares 2⅜″ × 2⅜″, then cut in half diagonally. You'll need 112 triangles for the Butterfly blocks (A).

Cut 12 strips 2″ × the fabric width, then cut into 224 squares 2″ × 2″ for the Butterfly blocks (B).

Assorted 1930s-style pastel prints

Cut strips 2⅜″ × the fabric width, then cut into a total of 56 squares 2⅜″ × 2⅜″. Cut the squares in half diagonally. You'll need 112 triangles for the Butterfly blocks (A).

Cut strips 2″ × the fabric width, then cut into a total of 168 squares (84 pairs) 2″ × 2″ for the Butterfly blocks (B).

Cut 56 C using the pattern for the Butterfly blocks.

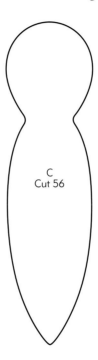

C
Cut 56

Appliqué pattern for butterfly body. Pattern does not include seam allowance.

Assorted pastel solids

Cut strips 2″ × the fabric width, then cut into a total of 168 squares 2″ × 2″ for the Snowball blocks (E).

Black solid

Cut a total of 2 strips 2″ × the fabric width, then cut into 26 squares 2″ × 2″ for the side triangles (E).

Assorted 1930s-style blue prints and solids

Cut a total of 116 squares 3½″ × 3½″ for the prairie points.

■ Piecing and Pressing

Use ¼" seam allowances. Press in the direction of the arrows.

Butterfly Blocks

1. Stitch assorted 1930s-style pastel print and off-white muslin A triangles together in pairs; press. Make 112.

Stitch triangles in pairs.

2. Arrange 2 matching units from Step 1, 3 assorted 1930s-style pastel print B squares, and 4 off-white muslin B squares in 3 rows as shown. Stitch the units and squares into rows; press. Stitch the rows together; press. Make 56.

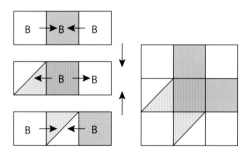

Stitch units and squares into rows, then stitch rows together.

3. Using the method of your choice, appliqué a butterfly body to each block. Use black embroidery floss to outline the body in a blanket stitch, and to add antennae with a stem stitch and French knots.

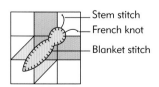

Appliqué and embroider butterflies.

Snowball Blocks

1. Draw a line diagonally, corner to corner, on the wrong side of the assorted 1930s-style pastel solid E squares.

2. Place 4 marked squares from Step 1 on each off-white muslin 5" square, right sides together.

3. Stitch directly on the drawn line and trim, leaving a ¼" seam allowance; press.

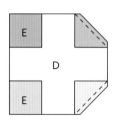

Place pastel squares on muslin squares and stitch on drawn line. Trim.

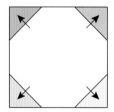

Make 42.

Side Triangles

1. Draw a line diagonally, corner to corner, on the wrong side of the black solid E squares.

2. Place a marked square from Step 1 on the right-angle corner of each off-white muslin F triangle, right sides together.

3. Stitch directly on the drawn line and trim, leaving a ¼" seam allowance; press.

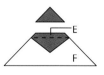

Place a black square on a muslin triangle and stitch on drawn line. Trim.

Make 26.

■ Quilt Top Assembly

1. Lay out the Butterfly blocks and Snowball blocks on point, alternating them as shown in the quilt construction diagram below. Finish with the side and corner triangles.

2. Stitch the blocks, side triangles, and corner triangles in diagonal rows; press.

3. Stitch the rows together; press. Your quilt top should measure approximately 45″ × 51½″.

4. Refer to Prairie Points on pages 22–23, and use the assorted 1930s-style blue pastel print and solid 3½″ squares to make 116 prairie points.

Refer to the quilt photo on page 40 and stitch the prairie points to the quilt top: 31 on each of the 2 sides, and 27 each on the top and bottom.

■ Quilting and Finishing

1. Layer, baste, and quilt your quilt top. Leave the outside 1″ free from quilting on all sides.

2. Refer to Prairie Points (page 22–23) to wrap the backing over the batting, and finish the back of your quilt.

3. Complete the quilting.

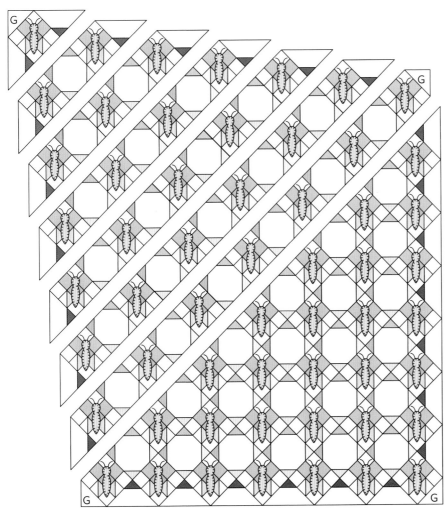

Quilt construction

Scrappy Triangles

Although it may look complicated, this scrappy quilt is very straightforward to piece using two simple nine-patch variations. The instructions tell you how many individual half-square triangles to cut, but you can substitute your favorite quick-piecing method to make scrappy half-square triangle units.

This quilt is 67" × 68½" and is made up of one hundred twenty-one 4½" blocks. An extra row of 1½" squares and half-square triangle units give the quilt its rectangular shape.

Fabric Requirements

Fabric amounts are based on a 42″ fabric width.

Assorted cream prints: 3 yards total for blocks, extra row, and outer border

Assorted dark red prints: 1¾ yards total for blocks, extra row, and pieced binding

Assorted medium and dark prints: 1⅝ yards total for blocks and extra row

Beige and cream stripe: ½ yard for inner border

Dark green print: 1¼ yards for vine and leaf appliqués

Assorted print scraps: 1½ yards total for flower and berry appliqués

Batting: 71″ × 73″

Backing: 4 yards

Cutting

Assorted cream prints

Cut a total of 281 squares 2⅜″ × 2⅜″, then cut in half diagonally. You'll need 561 triangles for the blocks and extra row. (You'll have 1 triangle left over.)

Cut 7 ½″-wide strips to total 250″ for the pieced outer border.

Assorted dark red prints

Cut a total of 281 squares 2⅜″ × 2⅜″, then cut in half diagonally. You'll need 561 triangles for the blocks and extra row. (You'll have 1 triangle left over.)

Cut a total of 7 strips 2⅛″ × the fabric width for the pieced binding.

Assorted medium and dark prints

Cut a total of 561 squares 2″ × 2″ for the blocks and extra row.

Beige and cream stripe

Cut 6 strips 2″ × the fabric width for the inner border.

Dark green print

Cut 1″-wide bias strips to total 300″ for the appliqué vine.

Cut 92 A using the pattern on page 47 for the appliqué leaves.

Assorted print scraps

Cut 36 each of B, C, and D; 24 each of E and F, and 52 of G using the patterns on page 47 for the flower and berry appliqués.

Piecing and Pressing

Use ¼″ seam allowances. Press in the direction of the arrows.

Scrappy Triangle Blocks

You'll need a total of 121 Scrappy Triangle Blocks: 61 Block A and 60 Block B.

1. Stitch assorted cream print and dark red print triangles in pairs; press. Make 561.

2. Arrange 4 units from Step 1, and 5 assorted medium and dark print 2″ squares in 3 rows as shown. Stitch the units and squares into rows; press. Stitch the rows together; press. Make 61.

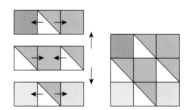

Block A

3. Arrange 5 units from Step 1, and 4 assorted medium and dark print 2″ squares in 3 rows as shown. Stitch the units and squares into rows; press. Stitch the rows together; press. Make 60.

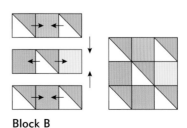

Block B

Quilt Top Assembly

1. Lay out the 121 Scrappy Triangle blocks, alternating Block A and Block B as shown in the quilt construction diagram. Stitch the blocks into rows; press.

2. Alternate the remaining units from Scrappy Triangle Blocks, Step 1 (page 45) with the remaining 2″ assorted dark and medium print squares to make the extra row along the bottom edge of the blocks. Press.

3. Stitch the rows together; press. Your quilt should measure 50″ × 51½″.

Adding the Borders

1. Join the 2″-wide beige and cream stripe strips end to end. (Since you are working with a striped fabric, you may prefer *not* to angle these seams.) Refer to Partial-Seam Borders (pages 11–12) to trim and sew the inner borders to the quilt top.

2. Stitch the 7½″-wide cream print strips end to end to make a pieced border strip approximately 250″ long. (I pieced these borders with straight seams as well.) Refer to Partial-Seam Borders to trim 4 outer border strips to the necessary lengths.

3. Appliqué 8 lengths of vine and pieces A–G to the outer borders. Refer to the quilt photo (page 44) to help with placement and Appliqué and Quilted Borders (page 14) as needed. Leave enough unattached vine to complete the corners. You'll cover the ends of each corner vine with a flower once the border is stitched to the quilt top.

4. Refer to Partial-Seam Borders (pages 11–12) to sew the appliquéd borders to the quilt top. Finish stitching the corner appliqué; press.

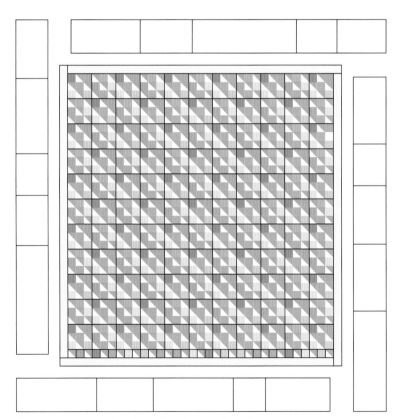

Quilt construction (appliqué border not shown)

◼ Quilting and Finishing

1. Layer, baste, and quilt your quilt top.

2. Refer to Double-Fold Binding (page 16) and stitch the 2⅛″-wide assorted red print strips end to end, with diagonal seams as described on page 8.

3. Refer to Mitered Corners (pages 18–19) and stitch the binding to the quilt.

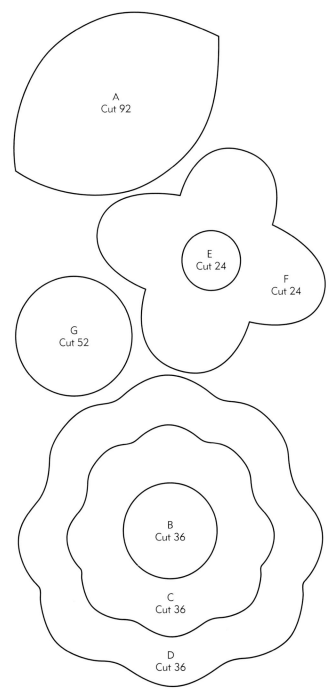

A
Cut 92

E
Cut 24

F
Cut 24

G
Cut 52

B
Cut 36

C
Cut 36

D
Cut 36

Appliqué patterns for *Scrappy Triangles* border. Patterns do not include seam allowance.

■ Index

■ About the Author

Alex Anderson's love affair with quiltmaking began in 1978, when she completed her Grandmother's Flower Garden quilt as part of her work toward a degree in art at San Francisco State University. Over the years, her focus has rested upon understanding fabric relationships and an intense appreciation for traditional quilting surface design and star quilts.

Alex currently hosts Home and Garden Television's quilt show *Simply Quilts*. Her quilts have appeared in numerous magazines, often in articles devoted specifically to her work.

Alex lives in Northern California with her husband, two children, two cats, one dog, one fish, and the challenges of suburban life. Visit her website at www.alexandersonquilts.com.

Other Books by Alex

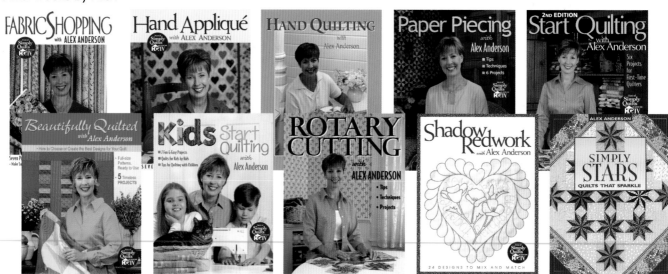